Craft Workshop

Fabric

Monica Stoppleman & Carol Crowe

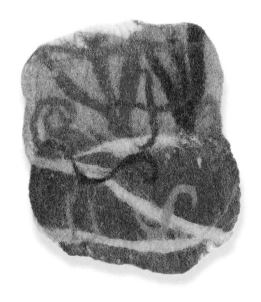

 Crabtree Publishing Company

Craft Workshop

Crabtree Publishing Company

350 Fifth Avenue	360 York Road, R.R.4	73 Lime Walk
Suite 3308	Niagara-on-the-Lake	Headington, Oxford
New York, NY 10118	Ontario L0S 1J0	England OX3 7AD

Edited by **Virginia Mainprize**
Designed and illustrated by **Mei Lim**
Photography by **Steve Shott**

Workshop leaders
Carol Crowe for the painted pattern, tie-dyeing and block printing workshops;
Francine Isaacs for the felt workshop;
Ali Rhind for the rug workshop; **Marcela Eldi de Persus, Karen Robins,**
and **Deb Todd** for the appliqué workshop.

Created by
Thumbprint Books

Cataloging-in-Publication-Data

Stoppleman, Monica, 1949-
Fabric / Monica Stoppleman & Carol Crowe.
p. cm. – (Craft Workshop)
Includes index.
Summary: Presents six different ways in which people from around the world work with and decorate fabric,
and then provides instructions for creating one's own craft projects using similar materials.
ISBN 0-86505-789-3 (pbk). – ISBN 0-86505-779-6 (rhb)
1. Textile crafts – Juvenile literature. 2. Textile painting – Juvenile literature.
3. Textile printing - Juvenile literature [1. Textile crafts. 2. Textile painting. 3. Textile printing. 4. Handicraft]
I. Crowe, Carol. 1951 - . II. Title. III. Series.
TT699.S78 1998   746--dc21   97-32137
                                              CIP
                                              AC

First published in 1998 by
A & C Black (Publishers) Limited
35 Bedford Row, London WC1R 4JH

Printed in Hong Kong by Wing King Tong Co Ltd

Cover photograph: This appliqué wall-hanging comes from Bihar in northeastern India. The scene
shows the goddess Durga with some of her attendants. Their shapes have been cut out of red
cloth, and are sewn onto a sacking.

Contents

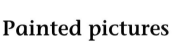
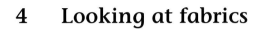

Looking at fabrics

Every day, people all over the world use fabric, or cloth, in many different ways.

In hot places, people wear cotton and linen to keep them cool. In cold climates, people dress in wool to keep warm.

People shape and sew fabric into clothes. They wind pieces of cloth around their body and head, like this.

In homes, fabric is used for decoration, comfort and warmth.

Fabric is made from thin strands, called fibers. For centuries, these fibers came from plants, such as cotton and flax, the wool and fur of animals, or from bark. Silk comes from the cocoons of silkworms.

Today, people also make fibers from other things. Acrylics are made from chemicals taken from wood. Nylon is made from crude oil pumped from the ground. These fabrics are called synthetics.

Fabric can be made several ways. Wool can be pressed and rubbed together to make felt. All fibers can be spun into long threads which are woven or knitted together to make cloth.

People have discovered many ways of bringing plain cloth to life. They dye it different colors, print it with patterns or embroider it with colored threads.

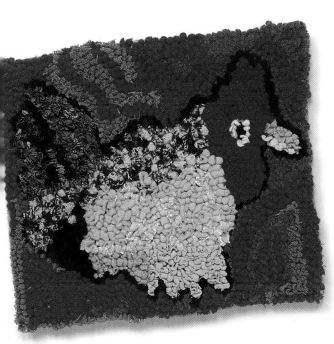

People have even found ways to recycle fabric. They cut up old clothes and use them to make quilts, rugs and wall hangings.

This book shows you ways you can work with fabrics and create your own fabric art.

Look at fabrics around your home, in stores, or in books and magazines. Start a fabric scrapbook. Collect interesting scraps of cloth. Copy patterns you like. Create your own designs using different colors and shapes.

Tools and tricks

General rules

• **Protect your work area with newspaper or a sheet of plastic.**

• **Wear old clothes or overalls.**

• **Carefully follow instructions for using dyes, paints and glues. Check it all with an adult.**

• **Keep a window or door open while you work.**

Fabrics

You will need different kinds of fabric for each project. Use only cotton or silk for printing, painting and tie-dyeing. Before you use new fabrics, wash them in hot water, dry them and iron them flat. Collect colored and patterned cloth for sewing appliqués. Try to find some woolen or other thick cloth for making rugs.

Dyes

Fabric can be colored by soaking it in colored liquid, called dye. You need only cold-water fabric dye and silk dye for the projects in this book.

It is important to dye fabric in a well-aired room and not to breathe in any dye dust. Wear gloves and perhaps a mask, especially if you suffer from asthma or eczema. If dye gets onto your skin, wash it off right away in cold water.

Use old plastic containers for mixing dye, as it may stain. For soaking fabric in dye, use an old plastic bowl. Make sure there is enough liquid to cover the fabric completely and use tongs or a stick to lift it out.

For tie-dying projects, soak the fabric in water before putting it in the dye. For fabric painting, use fiber active dyes or silk dyes. These are more expensive, but even a little gives a strong color.

Resists

To make patterns on cloth, you must stop parts of the cloth from soaking up the dye. One way of doing this is to protect those parts with a resist. Wax and gum are the most effective resists. Flour and water paste and liquid clay (slip) also work.

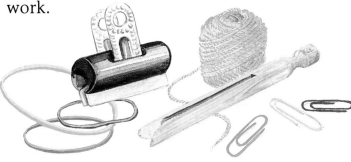

Another way to create a resist is to stitch, tie or clip fabric, so that dye cannot get through at those points.

Frames

Use a picture frame for painting patterns on cloth. With masking tape, attach the cloth onto the frame on all four sides, making sure it is tight and straight.

Small proggy rugs can be made on a picture frame, but for bigger ones, you will need to use a special rug frame which you can buy at a craft shop.

Printing blocks

Dyes can be stamped onto cloth with a solid object called a printing block. Make your printing block out of cork tile or thick cardboard. (Cork is better because it can be washed and used again and again). Use fabric inks or mix acrylics with textile binder to make your dye.

Here's a simple way to make your own printing block.

Cut two pieces of cork tile or thick cardboard to the same size.

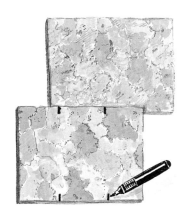

Draw a simple shape on one of the pieces.

Cut it out.

With waterproof glue, stick the shape onto the second piece of cork or cardboard.

Fabulous felt

The Kirghiz nomads of Central Asia travel with their animals, looking for new pastures. They live in tents and move from place to place, carrying everything they own.

fleece

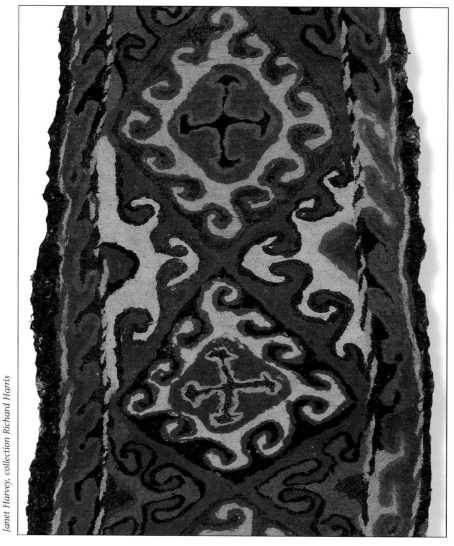

Janet Harvey, collection Richard Harris

carding combs

sheep's wool magnified 750 times to show the scales on a fiber

The Kirghiz nomads have made felt rugs, like the one above, for over 2,000 years. Felt is made from the wool and fur of animals. When the fibers are rubbed together in warm, soapy water, they make a flat sheet of felt.

Felt is known for its beauty and warmth. It can be used to make clothes, tents, rugs and even shoes. It is thick enough to protect against the sting of scorpions and other dangerous insects. However, fleas really love it!

To make felt, wooly fleece is shorn from sheep. The fleece is cleaned and brushed with combs so the fibers all lie the same way. This is called carding. Carded wool can be colored with natural dyes.

The carded wool is spread out on an old piece of felt, sprinkled with hot, soapy water and rolled tight. Kirghiz women roll this felt tube back and forth, pressing down hard with their arms. After a few hours, the wool inside the roll turns into felt.

Felt clothes are warm and waterproof. Shepherds in Central Asia wear long felt capes, which they use as sleeping bags at night.

The Kirghiz nomads live in large, round tents. The outsides are covered with sheets of undyed felt, which keep out snow, sun, wind and rain. The insides are decorated with brightly colored felt rugs, wall-hangings and cushions.

Felting fun

Making felt is simple and exciting. It is very wet work, so wear old clothes or an apron. Work outside, if possible. You will need some fleece and carded wool which you can buy from a craft or hobby shop.

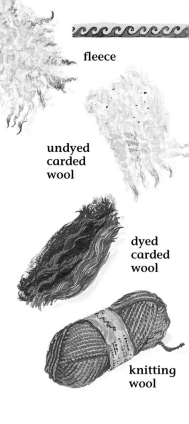

fleece

undyed carded wool

dyed carded wool

knitting wool

Little felt balls

Wind some thread tightly around a ball of fleece the size of a walnut. Wrap layers of colored, carded wool in different directions around the ball. Keep the wool in place with strands of knitting wool.

Put the ball in the foot of a nylon stocking. Tie the end with a slip knot. Dip the ball in hot (not boiling), soapy water, squeezing it over and over again until it becomes smaller and harder. Take the ball out of the stocking and pick at it with your finger and thumb. If no strands lift off, the wool has turned into felt. Rinse the ball in cool, clean water and squeeze it several more times. Let it dry.

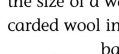

Felt jewellery

Make different colored felt balls and let them dry. Use a needle and string them onto a piece of strong thread. Attach fasteners to the ends of the thread.

A felt figure

With strong thread, stitch together two balls of felt for the head and the body. Make felt arms and legs and sew these onto the body. Sew on eyes, nose and mouth with colored thread.

Wooly wall-hangings

Arrange four layers of undyed carded wool in the center of a piece of thin fabric, such as gauze, muslin or cheesecloth. Overlap the pieces like roof tiles, laying the fibers of each layer in the opposite direction from those of the layer above. On the top, lay out a pattern or picture with colored pieces of knitting wool.

Fold the cloth around the wool and soak it with hot (not boiling), soapy water. Press and rub it hard all over with your hands or a rolling pin.

When the wool has flattened, press and rub the other side. Take off the cloth. Pick at the wool fibers with your fingers. If you can lift off any strands of wool, continue rubbing and pressing.

Once the felt is solid, wrap it around a stick and tie it in place. Sprinkle on warm, soapy water. Roll and press both sides on a hard surface. Rinse it well in warm water and roll the felt off the stick. Let it dry. Sew lines of stitching onto the felt to strengthen it.

Tie-dyeing

More than 2,000 years ago, people discovered that they could make patterns on fabric. They tied thread around bits of the cloth and dipped the whole piece in dye.

Monica Stoppleman

In West Africa, tie-dyed patterns are big and bold, as this cloth from the Ivory Coast shows. It was made of white cotton, dyed with the juices of plants and nuts.

Bits of the cloth are tied tightly so the dye cannot seep through. The cloth is made into long, flowing robes which show the whole design. They are worn by both men and women.

In India, both silk and cotton are tied tightly with thread. The cloth is dyed, and when the threads are cut, a pattern of tiny dots and circles appears.

This girl from Kutch, in western India, is wearing her wedding dress. Her silk veil has been knotted and dyed by hand. Hand-knotted cloth takes many hours to make and is worn only on special occasions. Machine printed cloth is used for everyday wear.

Ketuben Rabari/ Eleinud Edwards

The women who hand dye this cloth grow a long, pointed nail on their little finger. They use the nail to poke up tiny bumps of fabric.

Each bump is tightly tied with a thread that runs unbroken from bump to bump. The thread is left on until the cloth is sold to prove it was really hand-dyed.

Collection John Gillow

In Japan, fabric is folded and sewn to create beautifully decorated cloth. This woman is wearing a gown called a kimono. The ideas for the tie-dyed patterns on it came from flowers and waves.

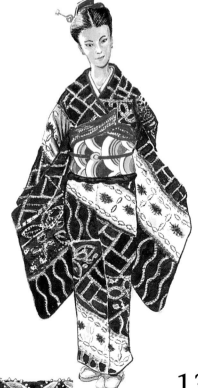

Dramatic dyeing

You can tie cloth in different ways to create different patterns. Choose the ones you want—wild splashes of color or more exact designs.

Fancy folding

Fold a square cloth in four. Roll it up and tie it in several places with rubber bands, as shown below. Soak it in clean water.

Put it in the dye bath for ten minutes and let it dry with the rubber bands on. For a different look, rinse the cloth in clean water and let it dry before you take off the rubber bands. When the cloth is dry, ask an adult to iron it. The outside of the cloth will be darker than the center.

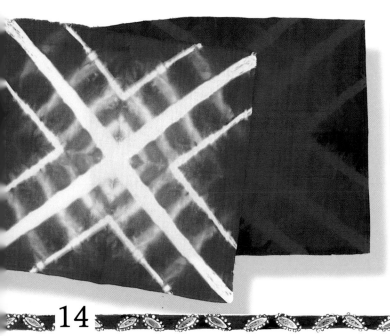

Surprise, surprise!

Roll a piece of white cotton fabric around a piece of string. Bunch it tightly. Tie the ends of the string together.

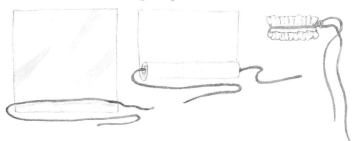

Soak the cloth in a dye bath. When you take the cloth out, keep it bunched up until it is dry. Untie the string. Ask an adult to help you iron the cloth smooth.

To get a different look, crunch up a piece of cloth and tie it up before you dye it.

Triangular folds

Fold a square of white cotton fabric in half to make a triangle. Fold it in half again and then in half once more. Attach clothes pins and paper clips to the sides. Soak it in dye and let it dry with the clips on. Iron it smooth.

Pleated folds

Fold a square cloth from side to side in pleats. Fold the strip from top to bottom in more pleats to make a square. Attach large paper clips to every corner or side.

Soak the fabric in dye. Let it dry with the clips on and ask an adult to iron it smooth.

Double dyeing

Tie-dye the same cloth twice. After the first dye, undo the folds. Let the cloth dry. Ask an adult to iron it so the dye won't wash out when you put the cloth in water again. Fold the cloth again in a different pattern. Tie and dye it a second color.

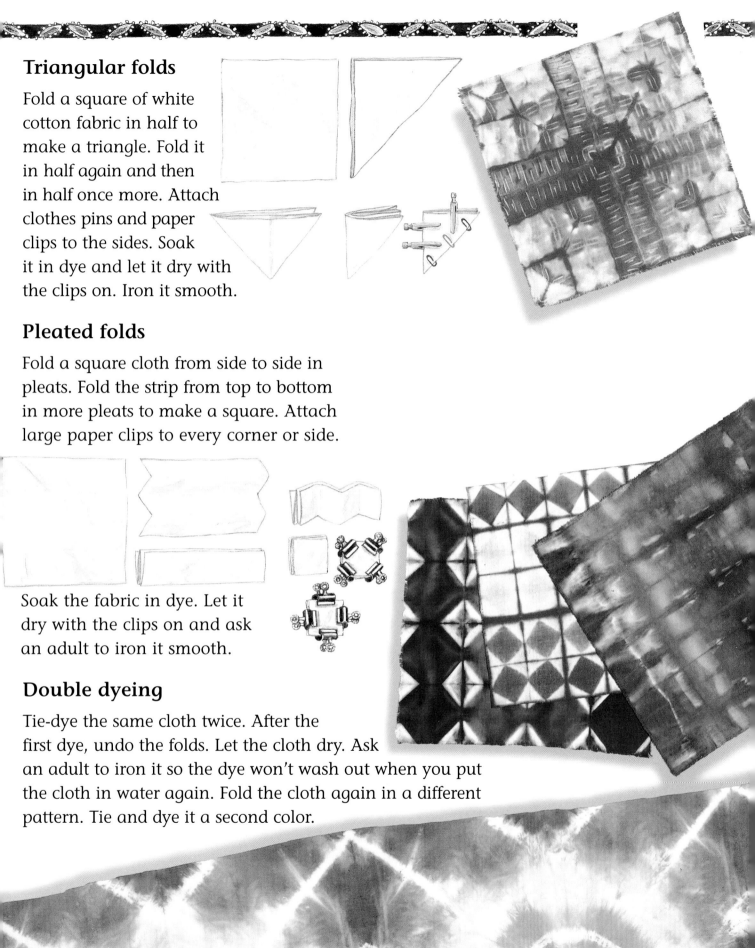

Painted pictures

This is part of an adire cloth which the Yoruba people of southwest Nigeria wrap around their body. Every cloth shows a Yoruba saying in pictures. The drawings on this cloth say 'my head is all together.'

cassava roots

indigo plant

wheel

duck

cocoa pods

wood-louse

Collection John Gillow

pigeon

key

stout bird

ostrich

The cloths are divided into sections. Artists paint on picture words which are part of the Yoruba writing. They are put together in different ways to give different messages.

A picture, such as this bird, on the back of each cloth is the artist's signature.

1 The blue dye used to color the cloth comes from the indigo plant. Its leaves are mashed into a pulp, which is shaped into balls and dried.

2 A dyer crushes fifty of these balls with wood ash in a large pot of water. After a few days, the liquid begins to stink. A blue scum forms on top. Underneath, the liquid is clear yellow.

3 An artist paints a design with cassava paste on white cotton cloth. The paste will stop the dye from coloring the parts underneath.

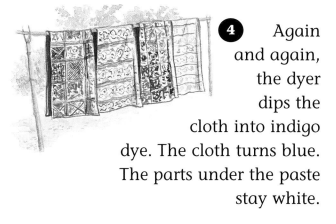

4 Again and again, the dyer dips the cloth into indigo dye. The cloth turns blue. The parts under the paste stay white.

Nicholas Barnard

This artist from Kalahasti, in Southeast India, is drawing characters from the Mahabharata, a Hindu story.
He draws lines of black gum with a bamboo kalam pen. As he presses the felt pad at the top of the pen, black gum runs down to the point.

The gum line acts as a resist. It stops the colors from mixing when they are painted on later. The finished cloths decorate the walls of Hindu temples.

In the past, the Japanese made banners with pictures of famous warriors and battles. Before a long piece of cotton was

dyed, pictures were painted on with rice paste.

This banner was made to celebrate the birth of a Samurai boy. It shows Yoiche, a legendary archer with his bow and arrow, winning a battle.

Fabric painting

It's easy to paint onto fabric to make pictures. You will be surprised by what you can do on your first try. The trick is to let the fabric soak up the color.

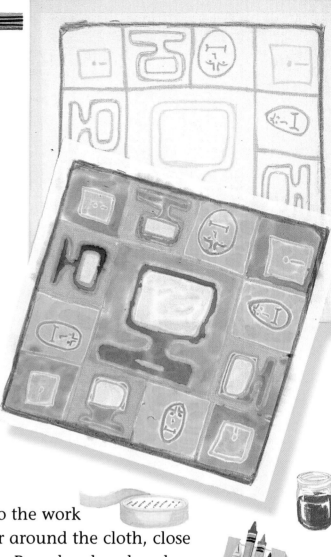

Personal pictures

Draw a simple design on paper. Repeat it several times to create a pattern. Plan the colors for your design. Tightly stretch white cotton cloth over an old picture frame and attach it with masking tape.

Lay down the frame so the cloth is next to the work surface. Using a wax crayon, draw a border around the cloth, close to the frame. Draw your design onto the cloth. Press hard and make sure there are no breaks in the lines. Dye will leak through any breaks. Put a layer of paper on top of and underneath the cloth. Ask an adult to iron the cloth on the frame, so that the wax melts into the fabric.

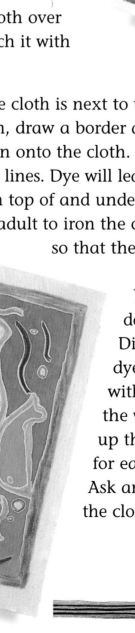

Turn the frame over so the cloth does not touch the work surface. Dip the tip of a brush into fabric dye and gently touch the cloth with it. Do not paint or go too near the wax lines. Watch the cloth soak up the dye. Use a separate brush for each color. Let the cloth dry. Ask an adult to help you iron the cloth.

Mythical figures

To paint pictures on silk, use a liquid gum called gutta.

Tightly stretch white silk over a frame and attach it with masking tape. With the silk on top, place your frame on a table.

Draw a gutta border on The silk and a figure from your favorite story in the center. Apply the gutta in unbroken lines. The dye will bleed through the breaks. When your drawing is finished, let the gutta dry. Dip the tip of a brush into silk dye and gently touch the cloth. Do not paint or go too near the gutta lines.

Let the picture dry. Take the silk off the frame. Put the silk between two layers of paper and ask an adult to iron it.

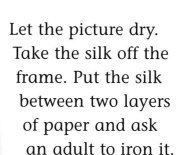

To remove the gutta, wash the cloth gently in warm, soapy water. Rinse the cloth and let it dry. Use your picture as a wall-hanging or for the front of a cushion cover.

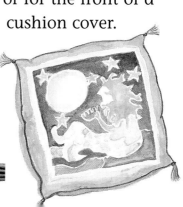

19

Block printing

The pattern on this Indian bedspread looks very complicated. In fact, there are only three different designs. Both sides of the cloth have been printed over and over again with three carved, wooden blocks.

Hindu motifs

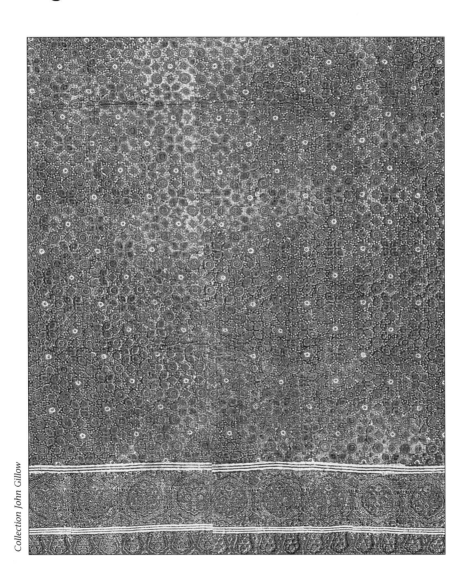

Collection John Gillow

Hindu motifs

For over four hundred years, cloths with patterns like these have been made by men in Kutch in western India. When these cloths were brought to England, three hundred years ago, they became very popular.

It takes fourteen separate steps to make this cloth. Undyed cotton is bleached in cow dung, softened with oil, dipped in tree sap, printed over and over with wooden blocks. Finally, it is dyed red, blue and black.

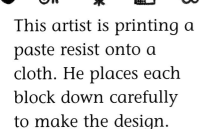

This artist is printing a paste resist onto a cloth. He places each block down carefully to make the design.

The paste must dry before the cloth is dyed. The parts of the cloth covered by the paste do not soak up the dye. The pattern is built up in many steps, using different blocks and colors.

Jabbal Khatri/ Eleinud Edwards

In Ghana, in West Africa, people make and wear cloth printed with pictures like the ones below. This cloth is called *adinkra*, which means 'farewell.' In the past, adinkra cloths were worn only at funerals. Today, people wear them for special occasions.

Each color has a special meaning. White means purity, joy and the spirits of the ancestors. Black is for death or very old age. Green is for new life and energy. Gray is for shame, and blue is for love. Red means anger and violence. Gold stands for the rule and power of the king.

Changing oneself
Playing many roles

Except God, I fear none
Symbol of the power of God

Moon and star
Symbol of royal blood and also means patience and faithfulness

The printing blocks are carved out of pieces of calabash gourd. Each symbol stands for a well-known phrase or saying. The symbols are always printed in black.

Adinkra king
Chief of all the adinkra designs. Means power and greatness

Collection John Gillow

Printing patterns

Turn plain white fabric into a beautiful cloth by printing it with patterns. Use things with unusual surfaces for printing blocks or make your own.

To make your own printing block, glue string or shapes cut from thick cardboard onto a piece of cork tile. Let the glue dry. (See page 7 for instructions for making printing blocks.)

To print repeat patterns, mark the back of your block with an arrow, to show the direction in which you are printing. Stick a loop of black, waterproof tape on the back of the block to use as a handle. You can turn the block to make different patterns.

Repeating patterns

Use fabric ink or mix acrylic paint with a little textile binder. Paint the dye onto a block. Press the painted block firmly onto some fabric—don't let it slide.

Print the same block again and again across the cloth or use two or more blocks with different colors.

To make a patterned border, print different blocks in a repeated order, around the edge of the cloth.

Mirror patterns

Make a row of prints on a cloth with one of your blocks. Turn the block in the opposite direction and make another row of prints right underneath the first. Repeat this mirror painting all over the cloth.

N

Compass patterns

Print your block with the top pointing north. Print it again with the top pointing east, then south, then west around an imaginary center point.

Try the same thing using different blocks and colors.

New cloth from old

In Peru, Chile and Colombia, women make
brightly colored wall-hangings and
bedspreads. They sew fabric scraps
onto a large piece of cloth.
This way of sewing is called 'appliqué.'

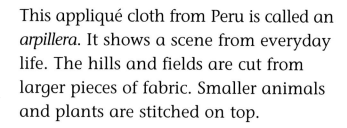

This appliqué cloth from Peru is called an
arpillera. It shows a scene from everyday
life. The hills and fields are cut from
larger pieces of fabric. Smaller animals
and plants are stitched on top.

The llama, cactus and fruit have
been padded to make them stand out
from the background. The people were
made separately and then sewn onto
the picture.

In the 1970s, the army in Chile overthrew the government and took away the freedoms of people. Many men were arrested and taken away, never to return. To honor those who had disappeared, the women made arperillas from their clothes.

Reproduced by permission of CAFOD

Each arpillera had a hidden message. This one shows a group of women walking to a center for homeless people. There are no men in the picture. The arperillo maker hoped that people outside of Chile would figure out the secret message and send help.

These figures are from a large appliqué made in northern India. The figures were cut out from pieces of fabric and sewn onto a plain background. The design was copied from wall-hangings which decorate the shrine of Salar Masud, a famous Muslim warrior. They tell the story of his winning a great battle.

Appliqué quilts have been made in North America since the 1600s, when America was a colony of England. The English passed a law forbidding colonists to make cloth. Buying cloth from England was expensive, so colonial women began recycling every bit of fabric.

Each week, women went to meetings, called quilting bees. They made appliqué squares which they sewed together to make friendship quilts. They were given to friends for special occasions, such as a marriage.

Cut-out pictures

Make an appliqué cloth with fabric scraps, gold and silver thread and bits of ribbon. Sketching your picture onto paper first will help you when you cut out the fabric pieces. The cloth will be in three layers—the background, the main figures and the fine details.

Appliqué animals

Cut out a piece of cloth for the background. On cardboard, draw the outline of an animal, large enough to fill most of the cloth. Cut it out. On a piece of plain or patterned fabric, draw around the animal shape with a felt-tipped pen.

Cut out the cloth animal and glue it onto the background. Glue on other pieces of fabric for the tail, ears, eyes, nose and mouth.

Dazzling disco

Show the excitement of a disco by using a dark fabric for the background, shiny fabric for the lights and ribbons for the light beams. Cut out dancers from plain fabric. Glue them onto the background. Decorate their clothes with tinsel and sequins. You can draw their faces with felt-tipped pens.

Cloth people

Pipe-cleaner people are simple to make. Twist two pipe cleaners together to make a shape of a person. Make the head, hands and feet out of cloth and sew them in place. Glue on bits of cloth for the eyes and mouth. Glue on clothes and some wooly hair.

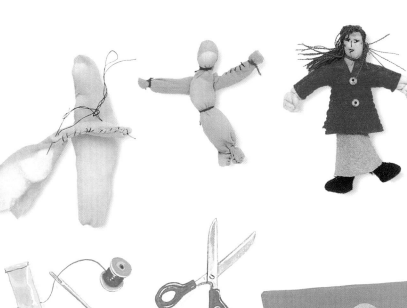

To make soft figures, stuff pieces of nylon stocking with cotton wool and sew them together. For the head, body and hands, wind thread around the neck, waist and wrists. Wrap pieces of cloth over the nylon body and sew the clothes in place. Glue on eyes, a nose and a mouth.

Real life drama

Think of an exciting story. Make a cloth picture of the most important part.

Cut out a large fabric rectangle for the background. Cut the main shapes out of brightly colored felt. Glue them onto the background. Make separate cloth people (see above) and sew them on top.

The picture above tells the story of a girl who fell out of her attic headfirst. An ambulance rushed her to the hospital where she soon got better.

Recycled rags

This wall-hanging was made by children and their parents with the help of an artist. They used hooky and proggy. These two old ways of making rag rugs had almost been forgotten. Today, they are popular again.

Ali Rhind

Proggy rugs are thick and shaggy. The strips of cloth are pushed through loosely woven fabric, called sacking. The rug maker pushes the strips from the back with a special tool.

Hooky rugs are made face up. Strips of cloth are pulled through sacking from the back to the front to make a flat rug. Hooky rugs have more detailed designs than proggy rugs.

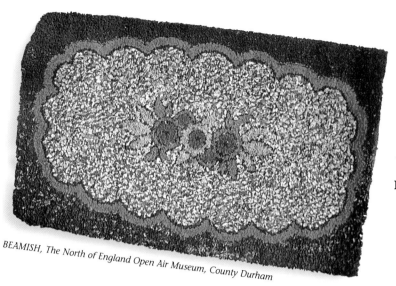

One hundred and fifty years ago, rag rugs were made in Scandinavia, England and on the east coast of the United States and Canada. Once people could afford to buy expensive woven carpets, they threw away their rag rugs. Today, few are left.

The whole family worked together to make a rag rug. Father made a heavy wooden frame over which he stretched cloth sacks. Mother drew designs on the cloth. On cold winter days, they made the rug. The children kept warm by the fire cutting rag strips.

An American farmer made this hooked rug in about 1850. With the burnt end of a stick, she drew the horse on a piece of sack cloth. Then she hooked the rug with pieces of worn-out clothes.

Perfect proggy rug

Make a thick, shaggy rug
to put beside your bed.

The frame and the progger

Ask an adult to help you tack 10 ounce sacking (you can buy this at a craft or hobby shop) to a wooden picture frame. Or buy a rug frame and follow the instructions for attaching the sacking. Make sure the sacking is tight.

Buy a progger or shape a wooden clothes pin, like this.

A bold design

Draw and color a design on a piece of paper. Use big, bold shapes which fill almost all the space. Mark a border 1½ inch (4 cm) from the edge of the sacking with a felt-tipped pen. Copy your design onto the sacking in chalk. Go over it with a thick, black felt-tipped pen.

Finding fabrics

Use pieces of thick fabric with texture, such as old woolen blankets, towels or denim and jersey. Try to find cloth of the same thickness. Cut it into 4 inch (10 cm) widths. Cut these widths into ¾ inch (2 cm) strips, as shown.

Push and prod

1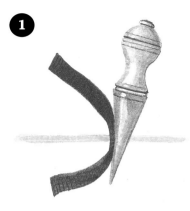

Rest part of the frame on a table with your design facing upwards. Holding your progger like a pencil, make a hole in the sacking and push one end of a cloth strip down into the hole. Catch the end underneath the sacking with your free hand and pull it half way through.

2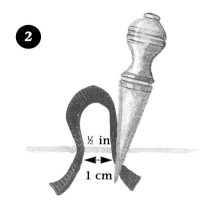

½ in
1 cm

Make a second hole about ½ inch (1 cm) away. Poke the other end of the strip through this hole, so that you get a flat loop on the surface facing you. Both the ends will poke out underneath the sacking. Check that they are about the same length. The underside of the sacking will be the top of the rug.

3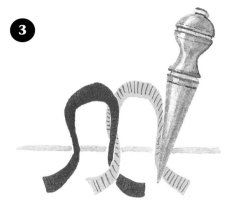

Push one end of the next strip into the same hole. Repeat the process as before until you have covered the space. Take the sacking off the frame.

4

Turn in the border of the sacking to create a hem. Sew it securely to stop the edges from fraying.

Turn your rug over and enjoy a big surprise! You can trim any long bits of cloth to make the rug more even.

Index

Acknowledgements

The authors and publishers would like to thank the following children for their help in testing and creating the projects in this book:
Kit Evans, Avril Fech-Stewart, Ryan Macleod, Sebastian Hendry, Iona Smith and all at Sychpwll for the felt projects; Ursie Allen, Sian Anthony, Georgy Ashcroft Spurr, Luke Baldwin, Sarah Barwell, Niki Baxter, Angus Beaumont, Grace Beaumont, Josh Blackwell, Liam Blackwell, Lizzie Blount, Elizabeth Breckles, David Bullivant, Ed Casswell, Alice Chan, Patch Coole, Jacob Coupe, Daisy Crook, Natalie Crookes, Ben Davies, Oliver Davies, John Dixon, Briony Gallimore, Laura Garbett, James Gibbs, Kayleigh Graham, Matthew Graham, Christopher Greenwell, Ben Gregory, Hayden Haslam, Brendan Jackson, Emma Johnson, Joe Labellarte, Murray Lockrie, Hinnah Mahmood, Maaria Mahmood, Daniel Mason, Laurie Matarasso, Briony Mcgeorge, Joe Naylor, Rosie Needham-Smith, Richard Newbold, Bethan Pearce, Judith Posner, Miriam Posner, Hassan Price, Ian Price, David Pritchard, Stephanie Purser, Thomas Sleep, Jack Smith, Imogen Sotos-Costello, Zoe Thomas, Jessica Thorpe, Lee Wade, Laura Wardel, Jenny Williams, Callum Young, Sammy Young and staff, in particular Ann Grierson, at Lady Bay Primary School, West Bridgford, Nottingham for the painted patterns, tie-dyeing and block printing projects; Camilli Bhogal-Todd, Izzy Butcher, Faye Gale-Robinson, Rosamund Hanson, Eva Garland, Milena Kelsang for the cut-out picture projects and Toni Suggins, Mark Cuthbertson, Lee Cox, Stuart Nairn, Sarah Coughlin, Helen Bulmer, Andrew McQuiggan, Gavin Rothery, Craig, parents and staff, in particular, Andrew Westerman, at Bournmoor Primary School Co. Durham for the rug projects.

They would also like to thank the following people for providing valuable information and loaning source material: Roy Russell and Mary Eve; John Picton; Mary Burkett 'the mother of felt'; Jeff Higley; Eleinud Edwards; Jeremy Farrell of the Nottingham Costume Museum; John Gillow; Mo Fini, Ali Shapter and Lucy Davies of TUMI; Jennifer Matthews; John and Helen Blackmore.

1 2 3 4 5 6 7 8 9 0 Printed in Hong Kong 7 6 5 4 3 2 1 0 9 8